Hawaii

EXPLORE THE UNITED STATES

Sarah Tieck

Big Buddy BOOKS
Explore the United States

One Nation

The United States is a **diverse** country. It has farmland, cities, coasts, and mountains. Its people come from many different backgrounds. And, its history covers more than 200 years.

Today the country includes 50 states. Hawaii is one of these states. Let's learn more about Hawaii and its story!

Did You Know?

Hawaii became a state on August 21, 1959. It was the last state to join the nation.

Hawaii is made up of a group of islands in the Pacific Ocean. It is the only state that is not part of mainland North America.

Hawaii Up Close

The United States has four main **regions**. Hawaii is in the West.

Hawaii does not have any states or other land on its borders. Instead, the Pacific Ocean surrounds the islands that make up Hawaii.

Hawaii has a total area of 6,468 square miles (16,752 sq km). About 1.4 million people live there.

REGIONS OF THE UNITED STATES

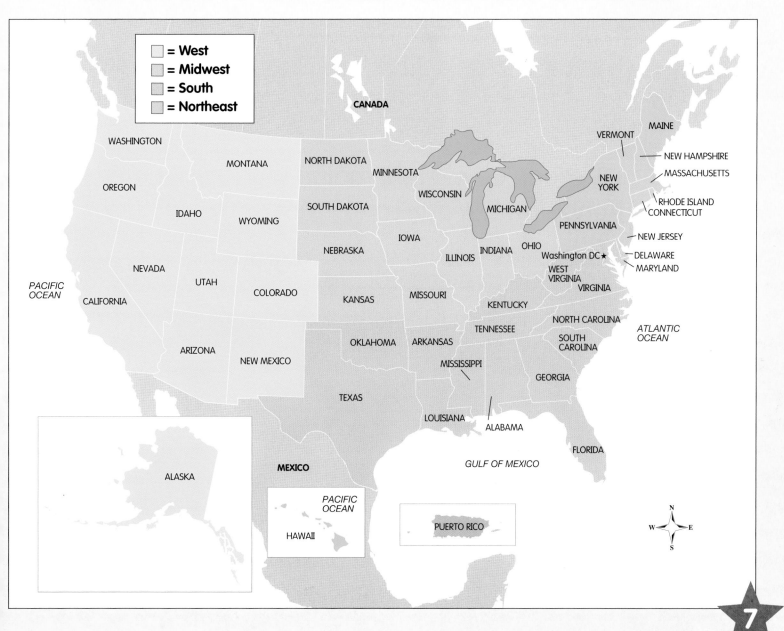

= West
= Midwest
= South
= Northeast

CANADA

WASHINGTON

MONTANA

NORTH DAKOTA

MINNESOTA

VERMONT

MAINE

NEW HAMPSHIRE

MASSACHUSETTS

OREGON

IDAHO

WYOMING

SOUTH DAKOTA

WISCONSIN

MICHIGAN

NEW YORK

RHODE ISLAND

CONNECTICUT

IOWA

PENNSYLVANIA

NEW JERSEY

NEVADA

UTAH

COLORADO

NEBRASKA

ILLINOIS

INDIANA

OHIO

Washington DC ★

DELAWARE

MARYLAND

WEST VIRGINIA

VIRGINIA

PACIFIC OCEAN

CALIFORNIA

KANSAS

MISSOURI

KENTUCKY

NORTH CAROLINA

ATLANTIC OCEAN

ARIZONA

NEW MEXICO

OKLAHOMA

ARKANSAS

TENNESSEE

SOUTH CAROLINA

MISSISSIPPI

GEORGIA

TEXAS

LOUISIANA

ALABAMA

FLORIDA

GULF OF MEXICO

ALASKA

MEXICO

PACIFIC OCEAN

HAWAII

PUERTO RICO

N
W   E
S

7

IMPORTANT CITIES

Hawaii is made up of eight main islands. These are Hawaii, Kahoolawe, Maui, Lanai, Molokai, Oahu, Kauai, and Niihau.

Honolulu is Hawaii's **capital**. It is on the island of Oahu. Honolulu is also the state's largest city. It is home to 387,170 people. It is a port city with many hotels and stores.

Did You Know?

Hawaii has a total of 132 islands. But, 124 of them are very small.

Oahu is the most populated island.

Hawaii

KAUAI

NIIHAU

OAHU

Pearl City
Honolulu

MOLOKAI

LANAI

MAUI

KAHOOLAWE

HAWAII

Hilo

N
W · E
S

Honolulu's Waikiki Beach
is a popular vacation spot.

9

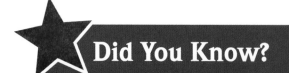

Pearl City is Hawaii's second-largest city. It has 47,698 people. Like Honolulu, Pearl City is also on Oahu.

Hilo is the state's third-largest city. It is home to 43,263 people. It is located on the island of Hawaii. Hilo is a port city on Hilo Bay.

Hilo is the largest city on the island of Hawaii.

Hawaii in History

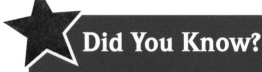

Hawaii's history includes explorers and royalty. **Polynesian** people were the first to live on the islands. In 1778, Captain James Cook arrived from England. Soon, Europeans and Americans began settling there. At this time, different areas were ruled by different chiefs.

By 1810, the islands were part of one kingdom ruled by King Kamehameha I. In 1900, the islands became a US territory. They became the state of Hawaii on August 21, 1959.

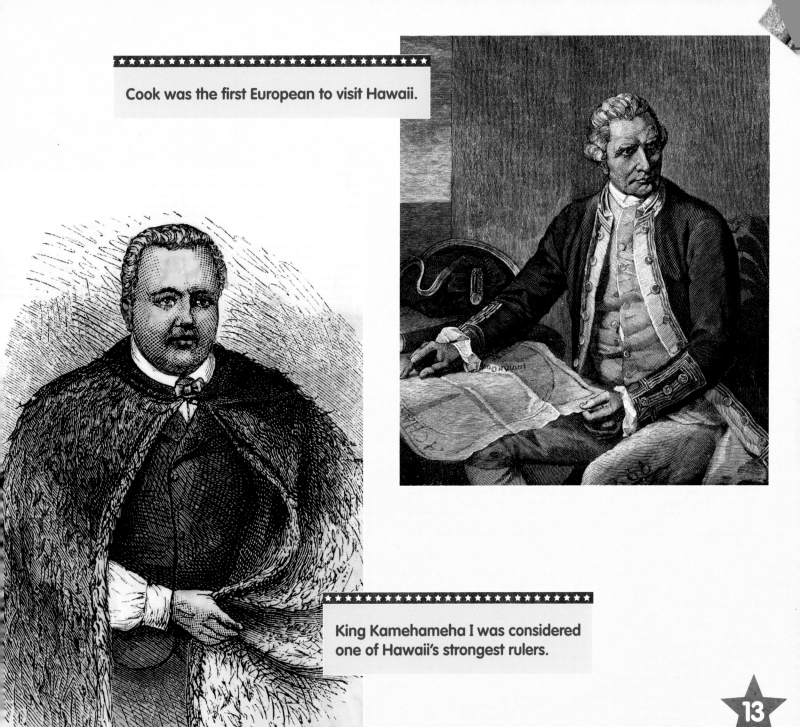

Cook was the first European to visit Hawaii.

King Kamehameha I was considered one of Hawaii's strongest rulers.

Timeline

1810

Hawaii's islands became one kingdom. King Kamehameha I was the first king to rule them all.

1893

A group of Americans and Europeans took power from Queen Liliuokalani.

1800s

Hawaii allowed the United States to build a naval base at Pearl Harbor.

Hawaii became a US territory.

1900

1887

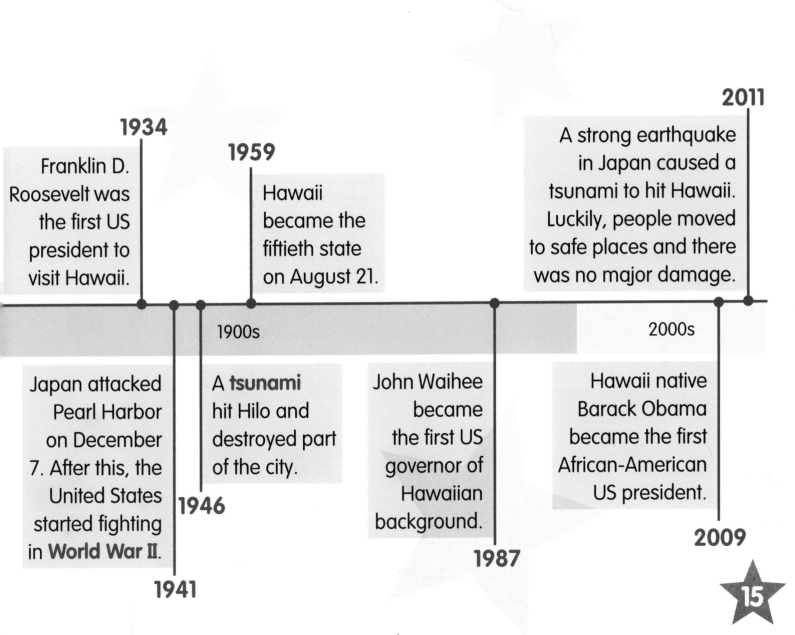

1934

Franklin D. Roosevelt was the first US president to visit Hawaii.

1959

Hawaii became the fiftieth state on August 21.

2011

A strong earthquake in Japan caused a tsunami to hit Hawaii. Luckily, people moved to safe places and there was no major damage.

1900s

2000s

Japan attacked Pearl Harbor on December 7. After this, the United States started fighting in **World War II**.

A **tsunami** hit Hilo and destroyed part of the city.

1946

1941

John Waihee became the first US governor of Hawaiian background.

1987

Hawaii native Barack Obama became the first African-American US president.

2009

Across the Land

Hawaii has caves, rain forests, waterfalls, **volcanoes**, and beaches. Mauna Loa and Kilauea are famous volcanoes on the island of Hawaii.

Many types of animals make their homes in Hawaii. The nene and honeycreeper are birds found only in Hawaii! Humpback whales and sea turtles swim off the state's coasts.

Did You Know?

Hawaii has warm weather all year. In July, the average temperature is 75°F (24°C). In January, it is 68°F (20°C).

Kilauea is part of Hawaii Volcanoes National Park. Lava often flows from it.

Rainbow Falls is near Hilo. It is in Wailuku River State Park.

17

Earning a Living

Hawaii is a popular vacation spot. So, many people have jobs that help island visitors. And, many US military members work in Hawaii.

Hawaii is also a farming state. Its farms and gardens produce different types of fruits and flowers.

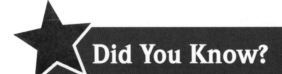

Did You Know?

Hawaii has to get certain needed products, such as lumber, from other places.

Hawaii's major products include pineapples (*above*),
orchids, papayas, ginger, coffee, and macadamia nuts.

Sports Page

Many people think of outdoor sports when they think of Hawaii. Swimming, running, windsurfing, and surfing are popular in the state.

Hawaii also has baseball and football teams. Many fans follow the University of Hawaii's football team. And, the Pro Bowl is played every winter in Honolulu. The country's most talented professional football players **compete** in this game.

Did You Know?

Vans Triple Crown of Surfing events happen in Hawaii each year. This is a major surfing competition.

Oahu's North Shore has popular surfing spots. These include the Banzai Pipeline, Waimea Bay, and Sunset Beach.

HOMETOWN HEROES

Many famous people are from Hawaii. Queen Liliuokalani was born in Honolulu in 1838. She is famous for being Hawaii's only queen.

Queen Liliuokalani ruled Hawaii from 1891 to 1893. Her rule ended when settlers from the United States and Europe turned against her. She was the last to rule the kingdom of Hawaii.

Queen Liliuokalani is remembered for writing a song called "Aloha Oe." This is Hawaii's good-bye song.

Barack Obama is another famous Hawaiian. He was born in Honolulu in 1961. In 2009, Obama made history. He became the first African-American US president.

Obama spent part of his childhood in Hawaii. He went to high school in Honolulu. As president, Obama worked to improve the US **economy**. He also worked with other countries.

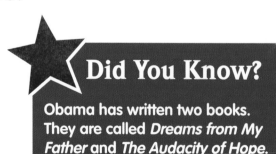

Did You Know?

Obama has written two books. They are called *Dreams from My Father* and *The Audacity of Hope*.

Sometimes, Obama visits Hawaii with his family. He and his wife, Michelle, have visited the USS *Arizona* Memorial.

Obama was the forty-fourth US president.

Tour Book

Do you want to go to Hawaii? If you visit the state, here are some places to go and things to do!

 **Swim**

Hawaii has many sandy beaches. Some of them have black sand! Swim, snorkel, or paddleboard in the water!

 Remember

Visit the USS *Arizona* Memorial at Pearl Harbor in Oahu. There, you can see where Japanese planes attacked US ships in 1941.

 See

Look for humpback whales! Some have babies near Hawaii in the winter months. These ocean animals can be more than 45 feet (14 m) long. And, they can weigh 40 tons (36 t)!

Taste

Many people attend luaus in Hawaii. At these special Hawaiian meals, people eat cooked pig. They may see hula dancers or hear Hawaiian songs.

 Discover

The islands of Hawaii were created millions of years ago from volcanoes. Visit Hawaii Volcanoes National Park to see active volcanoes.

A GREAT STATE

The story of Hawaii is important to the United States. The people and places that make up this state offer something special to the country. Together with all the states, Hawaii helps make the United States great.

Did You Know?

Aloha is a Hawaiian word with many meanings. It can be used to mean hello, welcome, love, and good-bye!

Hawaii is famous for its beauty. It has palm trees and colorful flowers.

Fast Facts

Date of Statehood:
August 21, 1959

Population (rank):
1,360,301
(40th most-populated state)

Total Area (rank):
6,468 square miles
(47th largest state)

Motto:
"Ua Mau Ke Ea O Ka Aina I Ka Pono" (The Life of the Land Is Perpetuated in Righteousness)

Nickname:
Aloha State

State Capital:
Honolulu

Flag:

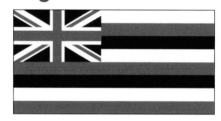

Flower: Yellow Hibiscus

Postal Abbreviation:
HI

Tree: Kukui

Bird: Nene
(Hawaiian Goose)

Important Words

capital a city where government leaders meet.

compete to take part in a competition, or contest between two or more persons or groups.

diverse made up of things that are different from each other.

economy the way that a country produces, sells, and buys goods and services.

Polynesian (pah-luh-NEE-zhuhn) a person from the islands of Polynesia in the Pacific Ocean.

region a large part of a country that is different from other parts.

tsunami (soo-NAH-mee) a group of powerful ocean waves that can destroy areas.

volcano a deep vent, or opening, in Earth's surface from which hot liquid rock or steam comes out.

World War II a war fought in Europe, Asia, and Africa from 1939 to 1945.

Web Sites

To learn more about Hawaii, visit ABDO Publishing Company online. Web sites about Hawaii are featured on our Book Links page. These links are routinely monitored and updated to provide the most current information available.

www.abdopublishing.com

Index